About the authors

Tim Arnold Famous marketer of the 80's and 90's who ran one of the most successful independent UK agencies. Going on to help establish a leading UK search marketing agency and become a sought-after interim Marketing Director and consultant.

Guy Tomlinson Leading UK marketing consultant with a background at major brands and in the media. Founder of The Marketing Directors, a successful research and marketing consultancy working with aspiring and global brands in the UK and beyond.

https://www.themarketingdirectors.co.uk/

THE

MARKETING DIRECTOR'S HANDBOOK

Volume 2

Managing digital marketing

Tim Arnold and Guy Tomlinson

The Marketing Directors Ltd

First published as a paperback in 2020.

Published by The Marketing Directors Ltd
Widmere Barn, Widmere Lane, Marlow, Buckinghamshire, SL7 3DF, England
Visit our website at https://www.themarketingdirectors.co.uk

Ordering Information
To order copies of The Marketing Director's Handbook contact your local bookstore, visit our website https://www.themarketingdirectors.co.uk, email handbook@themarketingdirectors.co.uk or telephone +44 (0) 1628 473699

British Library Cataloguing in Publication Data
A catalogue reference for this book is available from the British Library.
Arnold, Tim and Tomlinson, Guy
The Marketing Director's Handbook - Volume 2
Managing digital marketing

ISBN 978-0-9558860-2-7

Typeset in Ehrhardt MT, Gill Sans and Calibri
Printed and bound in Great Britain by Biddles Ltd., King's Lynn, Norfolk
This book is printed on acid-free paper responsibly manufactured from sustainable forestry in which at least two trees are planted for each one used in paper production.

Contents

Introduction

Change the World - Eric Clapton (1996)

Why read this book?

The Marketing Director's Handbook was developed to help the Marketing Director to not only direct and manage the marketing function but also to work with Boardroom colleagues to drive profitable organisation growth. As we said on the cover it is 'the definitive guide to superior marketing for business and boardroom success'. It's fundamentals remain bang on the money...

What has long held marketing back is a perception of fluffiness, partly linked to the creative function of the role, and partly to comparisons with empirically driven functions such as Finance and Sales.

Over the years, however, the importance of putting customers at heart of business has been proven in numerous studies, and evidenced in the out-performance of the most customer driven organisations (1). Marketing is thus increasingly recognised as a leadership function.

Further, as awareness of the profession grows, there are more degree-level courses available, and it continues to attract talent from clever, curious, analytical and creative people. Thus, fuelling further perceptual change.

Though 10 years on the landscape has changed irrevocably

We are in the digital age. And digital begets data.

The consequences are deep and profound. Some marketing functions have been reduced to the provision of digital services as the digital media platforms, including search engines, and social media networks, have plundered more than half the total advertising spend. Yet not one of them was created with advertising in mind.

Many digital marketing decisions are also driven by algorithms processing the data captured by these new media owners supported only by the information that they impart. Knowledge of the customer has been reduced to who searches for and who 'likes' what.

Yet, their decisions are sacrosanct.

Some see customers only as data to be exploited. Often flying in the face of the wishes of individual and organisation be it a company or a political party. Even the state itself is blithely patronised and ignored. Indeed, the Internet is awash with all of our information. Access to which is often sold unchecked, and customer control relegated to trawling reams of small print to uncheck the default settings that sell their personal details to the highest bidder. And business control is also relegated to amending the default settings that best serve the digital service providers.

Data and the numbers brigades from IT and Finance appear to reign supreme. External agencies have also declined in their influence, and digital specialists are simply that, with little overall strategic understanding. What expertise there is in digital markets has been acquired simply from immediate experience and operation. Thus, those making the decisions cannot understand 'what Marketing truly means' as process experts lack practical know-how of customer behaviour. As a consequence, the role of Marketing Director risks fragmenting and the function dissipating across customer service, sales and IT in the form of digital data management.

Yet much of the data comes from the digital empires themselves presented empirically as dictates of truth rather than algorithmic averages of their formulation. Words to match searches, targets to match profiles are mandated by them for best performance. However, they are not decided upon by meeting the brand's marketing aims or desired positioning, rather that which is already known. Which means marketing is based on uncertain facts rather than meaningful insights.

Loyalty has also become that which is searched for today. In the empires of the digital age, decisions are made to satisfy the emperor. Their processes beguiling yield: with what's promoted favouring most profitable advertiser click or distributor returns, pre-packed market comparisons limiting resistance to price rises, and what's served to whom based on the search engine or social media networks' judgement on the target.

In addition, apparently accurate decisions are also driven by organisational anomalies. The acquisition department pays for the cost of new customers, and the retention department watches over churn. Yet, the rate of churn is more important than loyalty which is managed by manipulating pricing and long contractual terms. Further, the focus on, and high cost of, customer acquisition through comparison sites at the expense of customer loyalty wipes out company integrity. It seems few see the big picture, and that long-term business building principles have been subjugated to short-term sales demands.

Creativity and value judgement have been devalued to the likes of 10 headlines that work. So, marketing becomes synonymous with processes which bring apparent success.

So what does this mean for the future of Marketing?

On one hand, we have more data-based consumer understanding but not on the customer him or herself. Also, creativity subservient to the budget, and a strategic overview and direction drifting away.

Yet, the digital world provides more channels, more promotion options, and more options to build brand equity.

So Marketing is once again at a fork in the road and the challenge remains; How to make Marketing more even effective, navigate the digital quagmire, and at the same time relate to the other functions, and lead the organisation?

It is our belief that although technology may have advanced the marketing fundamentals remain. Thus, the purpose of this new and fully up-to-date volume is to supplement our original work, help you better understand digital dynamics and manage Marketing in this digital age.

How to use this book

While this volume is a stand-alone, it fits like a jigsaw piece with other parts and chapters of The Marketing Director's Handbook. It is structured to help you undertake and manage specific digital marketing activities as well as the whole. For easy reference, the page numbering also follows on, and throughout the text, you will find sign-posts to other chapters, further reading and references (some with links to up-to-date digital data sources).

Managing Digital Marketing

Zeroes and Ones – Jesus Jones (1993)

In this chapter you will learn about:

- *The changing digital landscape*
- *Digital marketing strategies*
- *Success factors for search engine optimisation*
- *Success factors for search engine marketing*
- *Prominent digital and social media services*
- *Success factors for social media marketing*
- *B2C vs. B2B marketing*
- *Email marketing*
- *Mobile applications*
- *Integrated marketing*
- *Success factors for integrated digital marketing*
- *Marketing automation*
- *How to organise for digital marketing*
- *Managing the marketing function*
- *Pitfalls to avoid*
- *The future role of marketing*

Since the creation of the worldwide web in 1991, the world of marketing has changed. Expenditure on online search and digital advertising has grown steadily. In 2009 it exceeded expenditure on TV in the UK. Thus, the way we communicate and interact: the way we shop and entertain ourselves have irrevocably changed customer behaviour. Many believe that the fundamentals of marketing have changed irrevocably too. They have not.

The role of the marketing director in the digital world

Marketing has always embraced new media and developed new ways of understanding and influencing customer behaviour. Though the speed of change, and the technical complexity provide a constant challenge. The management of digital activity is also complicated by the way it is organised and delivered. Sometimes, by an in-house team, and sometimes by a supplier. Though usually by information technology and process driven staff who lack a wider appreciation of marketing.

In this chapter we discuss and provide insights to be a marketing director in the digital age. The role of the marketing director is to understand customers and create relevant brands to deliver growth. In the digital age the challenge is no different, just more complex. It represents an opportunity for the role to be re-asserted; providing the overview, developing the strategy, seeking out the best channels and media, understanding and interpreting the way customer behaviour has changed. While highlighting some of the technical nuances to fuel creative marketing and media solutions to attract and retain customers.

The changing digital landscape

In the 1990s ads were pre-planned and television dominated. Relationships with media salespeople were fermented over lunch. The retail multiples were on the rise and yet to reach the dominance they enjoy today. Amazon and ebay were not even gleams in the eyes of their founders. Back then business to consumer (B2C) marketing was primarily concerned with creativity delivered via a single TV film (known as a commercial). Industrial or business to business (B2B) marketing was seen simply as part of sales. The consideration, care and creativity lavished on a single 30 seconds ad; one film, one message, meant that it was, in effect, a brand builder. This message was then pushed out to a mass audience. Creativity and media buying were prerequisite skills for the marketing director. The media currency was cost per hundred advertising 'impacts' or gross rating points (GRPs), with impacts being the number of times an ad could be seen by a particular audience, multiplied by the percentage of viewers. The selection and relationship with the advertising agency, which often housed everything from research to PR, became particularly important as it was both the brand guardian and the marketing director.

Figure 31.1 *Changing digital landscape*

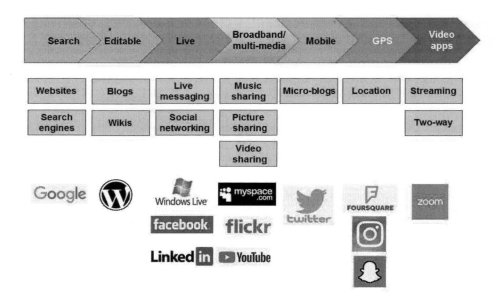

The worldwide web is a system of interlinked hypertext documents accessed via the Internet. In mid 2020 the number of indexed pages was estimated to be over 8.5bn (1). In the most advanced digital economies three-quarters of the population now access and search the web. Google launched in 1998, and though not the first Internet search engine, it has a dominant share vs. Bing, Yahoo! and Baidu in most markets. However, Google's share continues to erode (2).

In the mid 1990s editable websites, so-called blogs and wikis (3), evolved from on-line diaries, enabling easy online publishing and customer co-creation. The best-known blogging platforms are Wordpress (who claim to serve over 3 out of 10 websites) and Blogger (part of the Google family). Wikipedia is the world's largest 'wiki'. Those offering a more comprehensive service of domain name registration, hosting and site development have grown up. As have specialist providers in eCommerce and many other activity areas.

Invented by Microsoft, live messaging arrived in 1999. Originally cross-promoted with Microsoft e-mail applications, and known as MSN Messenger, it became Windows Live Messenger in 2005, and was subsumed into Skype in 2013. Enabling live text chat, this functionality remains part of many social media applications. Facebook, the world's largest social media application, providing live chat, personal social and affinity groups, gaming and multi-media sharing functions, launched in 2004. LinkedIn, the business-to-business equivalent, launched in 2003.

The introduction of broadband (high-speed internet connections) enabled large content files to be downloaded quickly. In turn this inspired new multi-media platforms including Flickr (photographs), My Space (music) and YouTube (videos). YouTube is now one of the world's most popular websites ranking in the top 3 in many countries in the world (4).

The growth of mobile and the idea of an individual using SMS messaging to communicate with a small group led to the development of Twitter (2006). This so-called micro-blogging service allowed users to communicate using an initial maximum of 140, though now 280 characters. Since 2015 it has also allowed the live streaming of video via Periscope. Fuelled by smart phone usage, Facebook also grew exponentially, their power and many uses even triggered revolutions.

Mobile phones with built-in GPS (global positioning satellite) functionality enable new location based services. Foursquare, a location-based service, then launched in 2009. This subsequently morphed into Foursquare Swarm. Mobile phone networks have also launched services to promote or advertise to consumers in specific locations. Like all forms of direct marketing this requires consumers to opt-in to receive promotional messages. This remains the main barrier to mass promotion via this medium.

The introduction of higher bandwidth mobile services (4G) (also known as long term evolution) enables seamless streaming of high-quality music or HD (high-definition) video on-the-move. Spurred also by the growth of mobile this then spurred many mobile apps with a photographic focus, as well as location tagging, most notably Instagram and Snapchat. Uploading photos to these social media networks or cloud storage now takes place in a blink. Voice command features such as Siri (iPhones) and Google (Android) are also more common-place and fuel more natural language search.

The most recently adopted technology is video mobile phone applications, such as Whats App, and now Zoom which enable both personal and group messaging and video calls. Growth has been spurred by enforced 'social-distancing' as a result of the 2020 Coronavirus pandemic; it has also become a default for commercial conferencing, as well as a mass broadcast medium.

Looking to the future all that is certain is that change will continue. 5G mobile will follow and ever faster broadband and fibre. Search algorithms will continue to change, technical constraints in terms of font and imagery will be liberated by new multi-media communications possibilities. Thus, higher creative promotion standards will be required.

The challenge for the marketing director remains to stay abreast of, and anticipate change, to gain an advantage over others.

Digital marketing strategies

Websites are no longer just a repository for information, acting as a shop window per se. They serve a broadening range of functions including promotion, entertainment, customer services as well as a place to shop. So as discussed in *Chapter 17 – Optimising Marketing Communications* view your website as *'Marketing Central'* (Figure 33.2). In other words, a hub for all marketing communication and relationship building activity, housing resources and downloads, and to enable customer interactivity, purchasing and service. All under-pinned by customer management, data storage and retrieval systems.

17

Figure 31.2 *The website as Marketing Central*

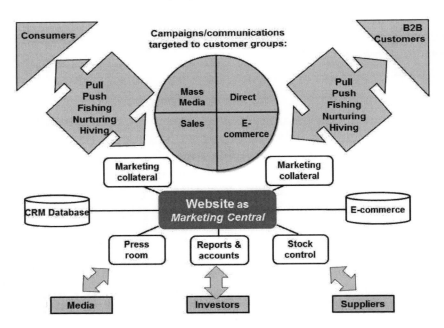

There are five broad types of marketing strategy to market and build your brand in digital space:

Pull: Involves attracting customers to your brand via the Internet i.e. optimising your website to attract search traffic (search engine optimisation (SEO)).

Push: Involves promoting your brand to customers via the Internet. Main vehicles include email marketing (electronic direct mail to customers) and online advertising including banners and videos. Pay-per-click (PPC) advertising or search engine marketing (SEM) are also forms of 'pull' marketing as they are influenced by search optimisation.

Fishing: Involves placing adverts, or embedding links to drive clicks to your website, or capture customers. Likened to 'fishing' in that 'nets' or 'squeeze pages' (4) are placed in locations where there are large shoals of fish, to attract or catch large numbers of customers. Co-opting affiliates or establishing price comparison sites or portals can be considered a form of 'fishing', whereby other fishermen, either individuals, businesses or high traffic websites capture customers. Fishing is also a form of 'push' strategy.

Nurturing: Involves building or buying a sales database and continuous promotion to engage and attract customers. This type of digital strategy sits between marketing and sales and is commonly used by B2B businesses. Nurturing is also a form of 'push' strategy.

Hiving (community building): Involves co-opting customers to a shared interest group or community. This enables relationship building with many people. This type of digital strategy is employed by both B2C and B2B businesses via major social media platforms, particularly Facebook and LinkedIn, as well as purpose-built platforms.

Search and Google - the elephant in the corner

Search is now a way of life and continues to change the way customers' source, select, and buy products and services. Internet search is a primary sourcing, selection and purchasing channel, a real-time check on offline or retail deals, and also a means for post purchase reassurance. The Internet is also a promotional medium and a medium to find promotions. For example, deals via price comparison sites, group offers via www.groupon.com, and extra cash-back via www.quidco.com.

Google dominates the search market though Bing, Baidu, and others, nibble away at this dominance. Its growth has followed the growth of the worldwide web and of search, though it did not set out to become an advertising medium. Consequently, its advice and tuition is concerned with the act of the search itself and not the relative performance.

Through the algorithms developed and used by Google, it determines the relative rankings of websites for all search terms as well as the relative value or cost of advertised search terms. Google is constantly evolving; adding new services and changing the nature of the search playing field. Only in 2011, for example, did the scale and activity in social media, become searchable.

Looking to the future (at least for those who do not regularly clear their cookies or are signed-in to a Google account), personalised search, where your past search informs your future search, is increasingly taking over from the simple banner and link. Search is also influenced by separate, often competing sources. The concentration on searched for words, links and 'likes' or ratings that Google's computers prefer is vital to building and running a website.

Search engine optimisation

Building websites presents the marketing director with the challenge of balancing technical skills with design while also optimising for operational search relevance and usage.

In parallel digital has raised the quality of the online customer experience, photographic images, literature, animation and movies. It has also altered the search playing field meaning that two skill sets are required to create compelling and easily discovered online experiences. Finished art and typography must be devised and embedded to web standards to maximise search engine rankings and deliver motivating customer experiences. Whilst copy and content must satisfy the twin demands of search suitability and brand values.

 Success factors for search engine optimisation

Understand your customer

Whilst the search engine operators provide a rich array of analytics information to identify the important search terms, it provides no diagnostics on *why* terms are searched for or *how* a website is perceived. The amount of customer and search information provided is also reducing in part linked to increasing privacy protection.

The only way to drive online awareness and demand for your products or services is to put the customer at the heart of your decision-making process. Use research to understand your different customer types and needs, how they become aware of, consider and purchase your product or service. In particular, understand the role of the website and other digital media in their journey, the search terms used, and the content, functions and experience that enable you to stand-out against your competitors.

Understand how Google's algorithms work

You may well rely on a specific managers or external agencies, however the more you understand how Google operates, the more successful you will be. The precise nature of Google's algorithms is known only to Google. Further, the algorithms change *frequently*. However, some knowledge is in the public domain via teaching materials, and industry research. Google's broad aim is to promote the best sites at the top of the search engine results page and demote poor-quality sites. Google employs raters to assess sites for quality, and this starts with analysing the *intent* of search queries. According to Google there are four types of search queries:

1.   *Know* queries; searching for *specific information.*
2.   *Go* queries; searching for *specific pages.*
3.   *Do* queries; searching *to buy or do something* such as play a game.
4.   *Combination* searches; searching to accomplish two or three of the above goals.

Searches which satisfy the most *common intents* are rated most highly.

Search utility, or fitness for purpose, is the most crucial component of search engine quality, with utility assessed by Google on the following best-to-worst scale:

*   Vital: When a specific landing page is the purpose of the query.
*   Useful: When a url (web page address) *satisfies* the main purpose of the search. Useful pages are also deemed to match some of the following descriptions: authoritative, entertaining and/or recent, be 'well organised', clear, trustworthy, and not 'spammy'.
*   Relevant: When a url is average to good, but not very good. In other words, they may be helpful for many or some users.
*   Slightly relevant: A page is considered slightly relevant when it has outdated, low-quality or copied information or too specific or too broad content.
*   Off-topic or useless: This rating is given to pages unrelated to the search query. Pages will lack content and may be stuffed with links or ads.
*   Unratable: This lowest rating is given to pages that cannot be evaluated. For example, because they are in a foreign language, fail to load or contain error messages.
*   Spam flags: Pages designed with deceptive techniques such as hidden text, keyword stuffed urls, are also downrated or dropped from the index.

So, transform relevant pages into useful pages through basic optimisation. For an up-to-date view on what this means in practice, https://moz.com and www.seomoz.org are good places to start. Moz surveys SEO professionals biannually, and asks them to 'weight' the importance of various ranking factors. The results of their most recent survey are summarised in Figure 31.3. Each 'area' was rated on a likert scale of 10, with 1=not influential and 10=highly influential.

Figure 31.3 *Weighting of SEO Google Ranking Factors*

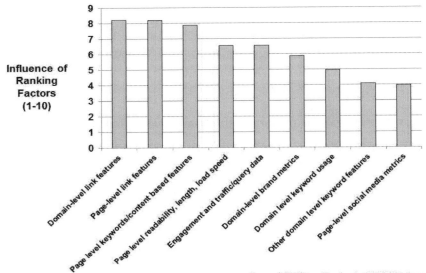

Base: >150 SEO professionals, SEO MOZ, August 2020

Establishing links to your website page is widely viewed as the most important ranking factor. So, establish links from other web pages using your chosen keywords. Prefer to link from more authoritative domains and pages, so-called high-level domains, and pages, as these confer more credibility to the link, and thus Google will rank the page more highly. Conversely, avoid linking from poor sites or so-called content farms. These are seen as superficial and downgrade rather than upgrade page rankings. Quick ways to do this are to register on local directories, and to comment on posts on high ranking influencer blogs.

Also build links to your most important pages from within your own website, as this also guides Google to feature these most prominently.

Page-level keywords and content-based features indicate the incidence of keywords on a page or in associated page meta data. When designing webpages, build relevant keyword combinations into specific pages, and also include related variants. Aim for around 1.5% incidence in the body text as too high or too low will cause your ranking will suffer. These should also be reflected in the website page name, paragraph headings and body text. Also, the page title, meta-description and image (alt) tags.

Other page-level features to address are text readability, uniqueness, load speed, structured data, and HTTPS. To boost readability, write as you speak, using natural language. Prefer shorter sentences, words of fewer syllables. In turn, this boosts readability for voice search.

Page load speed is influenced by files sizes, both code and images, and users prefer fast loading pages. Thus, aim to minimise file sizes to maximise load speed. To maximise speed, you also require good hosting, good underlying software (and we won't get too technical here), and to minimise the load on servers. Help is at hand in the form of website plug-ins. They variously minimise images, better manage or accelerate page loading or cache your website pages. Accelerated Mobile Pages (AMP) presently speed mobile delivery, though Google suggests its days are numbered. So keep an eye on Google news feeds and for their advice on the latest best practices (5). Also use Google's Page Speed Insights test to assess your page load speed and identify improvement opportunities.

HTTPS (Hypertext Transfer Protocol Secure), rather than 'plain' HTTP based sites, also influence ranking. HTTPS sites are encrypted by Transport Layer Security (TLS) and only cost a few extra pounds in hosting fees.

Engagement and traffic/query data include visitor traffic/usage signals such as click-through rates, time on site and page views. According to Moz, 'bounce' rate (the percentage of visitors who only visit one page) does not strongly correlate with a high search performance though tread carefully as this seems counter-intuitive.

Domain-level brand metrics reflect the offline salience of your domain or brand, for example, in the news and press, or via awareness created by longevity and advertising.

Other domain level features include the domain name length, name, and nature of SSL (Secure Sockets Layer) certificate (an encryption-based Internet security protocol).

Finally, page-level social metrics relate to the quality and quantity of social media mentions. Thus, as well as establishing your own social media sites, and links back to your website, build a steady flow of quality posts, shares, or retweets (Twitter), and likes back to your pages. Google Local Business encourages this at least every 2 weeks.

Understand search demand

When designing or optimising a website start by understanding where search demand lies; as choosing a low demand keyword suggests even if you rank #1 on Google, traffic will be low. The Keyword Planner in Google Ads is a boon to this end, providing demand by a geography, time period, as well as an indication of how competitive it is for a particular term. Then use this know-how to structure your website. Figure 31.4 summarises UK search demand for terms associated with marketing companies, agencies, and consultants.

Figure 31.4 *Search demand for marketing companies*

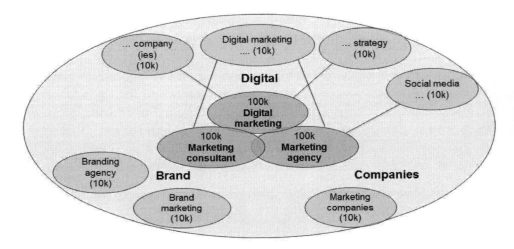

Source: Google (12 months to Feb 2020)
Mean monthly searches in UK

At this level of analysis there are 3 main clusters of words: marketing consultant, marketing agency and digital marketing, with a handful of related, yet discrete terms, in the areas of branding, companies, strategy, and social media. These provide insights on how customers think, segment and delineate the market. These then provide start-point insights to focus both offer and website development.

Moving forward the challenge is to create an original offer, or brand, and then page content to promote your brand and match user needs.

Think like a media brand

Google rewards original content. Content that interests, prompts customers to click-through, read, and delve deeper into a website are deemed to satisfy. So, aim to maximise customer satisfaction in terms of time on site and page views

Beyond your own website, building blogs and writing articles with links to your web page, is a relatively low cost and effective way of driving traffic, and boosting a site's ranking. Websites or blogs built using platforms such as Wordpress also means that adding pages multiplies the number of page links.

Continuous trial and error

Continuous trial and error should be part of your website optimisation strategy. We call this the 'Painting the Forth Road Bridge' type of marketing; when one coat has been applied, apply another to keep the paint fresh, and prevent rot.

However, not all is intuitive, as Google algorithms, by definition, make trade-offs. On one hand, Google rewards fresh or frequently changing content, yet it also rewards original content. Yet both cannot be equally important. Thus, benchmark your performance vs. other leading websites in your category to reveal opportunities for improvement and stay ahead of the rest. This also mitigates against changing algorithms.

 Best Practice

The Marketing Directors run continuous experiments to boost our search engine ranking; try searching for 'brand marketing consultancy', 'strategic marketing consultancy' and plain 'marketing consultancy' to see how well we're doing! We find the Search Console one of the most valuable tools to focus our traffic building effort. Checking the 'performance' report will tell you the volume of clicks and impressions for specific search terms or queries, and thus your market share for those terms. Further investigation will tell you the average position for those terms, and the pages on which the term appears. So use this information to focus your website optimisation effort.

It is also likely you'll find high ranking terms that you did not expect. With this information, you can better optimise your pages for those terms. So first check who ranks above you for those terms and why. Then rewrite your text to better meet a search intent, add more content, or build more links to that page using the same term. Though as Google algorithms force trade-offs, ongoing trial and error remains vital to optimise search performance. So only make one or two changes each time in order to delineate and truly understand what works and what doesn't. This also allows you to reverse changes if and when they have a negative ranking effect.

Use Google and other free analysis tools

Google also offers a number of useful website analysis tools so make the most of them:

- <u>Google Analytics</u> contains functions which allow side-by-side page tests to measure the effect of changes to a web page. So monitor the search traffic, as well as page click-throughs, to identify the best performing pages and page variants.

- <u>Google's Search Console</u> provides insights on the number of indexed pages, links to sites, search term volume, ranking and your share. These help guage a website's place in the market and where you could gain extra share of clicks. It also provides insights on the share of specific search term traffic that specific pages get, as well as their ranking. This is invaluable information to boost your website performance for specific keywords.

- <u>Google's Page Speed Insights</u> gives a 'speed' rating for mobile and desktop websites, on a scale from 1 to 100. It also covers Google's page experience factors, including so-called 'Core Web Vitals' due for inclusion in Google's search algorithms from the second half of 2021. As well as providing a 'score, this site provides lots of diagnostics and advice to improve your page speed.

The market is flooded with many 'experts' who offer services to improve SEO or raise the effectiveness of PPC. They aim to circumvent the structure of Google for their clients' benefit. However, in practice, many professionals are self-taught, and their skills have to be questioned. Software programmes also exist to match the algorithms and replicate the ranking and bidding process. Some such as Yoast, initially only available for Wordpress sites, are now available for multiple platforms, and in free and premium versions. The marketing director cannot go far wrong using free knowledge, tools, and skills, though otherwise needs to shop wisely.

Search engine marketing (Pay-per-click)

Pay-per-click advertising is dominated by Google Ads (formerly Adwords) and Microsoft Advertising (formerly Bing Ads). Though Facebook/Instagram, Twitter, YouTube, Amazon and others are increasingly getting in on the act and offer ever more sophisticated ways to both target and promote to audiences.

For Google and Microsoft, the price is set both by volume and bid. The blind auction format means that as demand for a search term increases, the more expensive it gets.

Planning involves determining key search terms with spend set by budget - either price per click or budget per day. Google, compared to the ITV companies of old, does little to husband clients or encourage specific spend. Planning and monitoring is based on historic data - simply a record of clicks or behavioural outcomes, unallied to the company, its brands or its customers. Yet there are some simple rules to navigate the quagmire.

 ## Success factors for search engine marketing

Understand how Google's algorithms work

The rules that apply to optimising your PPC ads to drive clicks appear similar to, but are not the same as, those that apply to optimising your website for search! Further, the systems are far from intuitive, and change frequently. So again, tread carefully.

Start by understanding how Google's keyword quality scores work. Google introduced quality scores for keywords, ostensibly to offer a better bid value, but they only reinforce the already explained practices of searched for words and related content with links to a web page and overall site traffic. Keyword quality scores range from 1 to 10. A high-quality score means that there is a high match with the keyword searched for, your advert and the landing page to which the advert link is directed. The benefit of a high-quality score, say 8.0 means that you will potentially pay half the price for a click compared with a competitor who has a keyword quality score of 4.0. Our initial experience, as a specialist strategic marketing consultancy, was that it was possible to achieve a 10-keyword quality score for ads directed to our home page. Over the years, however, this became ever more difficult on Google Ads, while straightforward on Microsoft Ads! This led us to question the sense of Google's algorithm, and thus reduce our investment in the medium.

Secondly, understand the difference between keyword match types, of and the pitfalls associated with those match types. There are four main match types:

- Broad match: The default, whereby Google's algorithms seemingly trigger your ad to show for anything related to your choice of keyword. Naturally, this delivers the highest volume of impressions.

- Modified broad match: Using the + signifier, for example, +dress, tells Google that the search query must include the term 'dress'.

- Phrase match: Adding double apostrophes around a term, as in "black cocktail dress", allows your ad to show only when a browser types in the same phrase though in any context. Thus, your ad would show if preceded or followed by other words, such as "how to clean ....", ".. for Barbie dolls". Nowadays, Google also allows plurals to show.

- Exact match: A few years ago, this term only appeared when browsers typed exactly the same term [Lake District camping]. However, nowadays phrases that Google considers the same intent also trigger an ad to show. Thus, for example, 'campsites in the Lakes' would also trigger an ad to show as would many other variants.

Therein lays the pitfall with Google Ads. Our own experience, as a marketing consultancy, is that less than 1 in 4 searches match *our* desired intent – to attract more enquiries and clients! There are many searches which Google considers the 'same intent' that we do not agree with. These include folk who wish to sell to us and job seekers. Also, general knowledge seekers, for example folk wishing to know 'what is a marketing consultancy?'.

A partial solution to this issue is to 'set' negative keywords to prevent your ad showing for what you consider a wrong intention. Thus, at the last count we blocked over a thousand terms, including many overseas destinations, and lots of job, and employment terms!

Customers buy benefits

While not rocket science, this point is easily overlooked in digital marketing. The basic marketing communication principles remain the same. Customers buy benefits. The more compelling and distinctive the benefits offered, the more likely your message is to persuade. So, to labour the point – make sure that the differentiating *benefits* of your product or service are crystal clear in your ad copy – and avoid the trap of just promoting *features*. Hard-won experience of writing PPC advertising copy really does show that the most benefit laden ads work best. If you have the ability to promote one, two or three benefits – do not be surprised if the latter is most effective. For a refresher on the difference between benefits and features take another look at *Chapter 7 – Product Strategy.*

7

The importance of measurement

The land of digital is affected with a form of myopia. We possess the data, yet the data is only a behavioural analysis of on-site visits and action taken. It is historical. You do not drive forward using only your rear-view mirror, so just focusing on past activity means it is of limited use as a predictive or planning tool. What is also lacking is understanding – an explanation of the reasons for behaviour or differences between various groups of customers.

Inability to understand the appeal of messages to target customer groups, and inability to understand the reasons for click-through-rates (CTRs) compound the difficulty in campaign analysis and planning. Consequently, it is not even attempted by most. Yet this know-how is vital to effective campaign planning and management.

The judgement of Google, its outpourings of what 'words' are best to buy, and the results, is all based on algorithms - a set of judgements, guesstimates or anticipations. These algorithms are translated into the rules of the software programme which, apparently, becomes sacrosanct empirical data. As marketing director, your role is making investment decisions based on comprehensive understanding and facts.

Where to start

As with all advertising, success comes from understanding your customers and effective communication planning. In other words, reaching customers at a time, and in a place, that is most likely to prompt a purchase. Then buying media at the lowest cost and measuring and investing in what delivers highest returns.

Understand your customer groups

The use of digital media is largely inversely proportional to age. With younger and more upscale males being more 'tech savvy' and also the most typical technology 'early adopters'. Yet there are even differences between so-called 'Millennials' (those born between 1981 -1996) and 'Generation Z' (those born between 1997 and 2012). Millennials watched digital innovation begin yet Generation Z were immersed in it from the day they were born. So start by understanding your customers. As well as demographics, understand psychographics, their needs, attitudes and behaviours, and use these to model customer groups or segments. Some ways to do this are discussed in *Chapter 6 on Customer Strategy.*

6

Understand the customer journey

Second understand the journey that each of your customer groups takes to discover and engage with your brand.

This requires qualitative research to observe, challenge and truly understand customer's behaviour and attitudes – and the drivers and barriers to discovering your brand, and activating demand

The more you learn, the more you will understand where, when, and how to persuade. A summary of the steps on a customer journey and an example journey in the travel industry is shown in *Chapter 6 Customer Strategy*. Conversely, in the online world, customers are attracted, and engaged in a non-linear fashion (Figure 31.5). This highlights the benefits of employing 'fishing' strategies i.e. deploying your 'bait' and 'fishing-nets' to attract and capture shoals of customers wherever they are. Google coined the term, 'the messy middle' to describe this part of the journey. According to Google's recent research, promoting your brand in relevant places is sufficient to switch up to one third of demand from the customer's favourite brand in a category to a less favoured brand (6).

Quantitative research is also useful to quantify the importance of drivers and barriers, the volumes of customers consuming specific media, and thus prioritise particular marketing strategies or tactics.

6

Figure 31.5 *The online customer journey*

Determine keyword clusters

Again, use the Google Keyword Planner to determine popular search term combinations and the volumes of those terms. Then, codify these into clusters of similar terms, to focus a PPC campaign. The narrower the group of terms in a search campaign the easier it will be to create advertising messages that match the sense i.e. customer intent, behind those terms. As a consequence, this helps to maximise keyword 'quality' as defined by the search advertisers, and in turn, reduce costs per click.

Establish campaign tests

A practical way to test and optimise PPC advertising is to establish a series of individual campaigns, each focused on a small number of *similar* keywords. To keep things manageable, create no more than three different adverts focused on a handful of keywords. Then, over-time, monitor performance and keep removing the weakest performing ads, and replace it with a new ad based on the lessons you learn. But do not just base your decision making on click-through rates alone. Monitor bounce rates, depth of visits to a website, and ultimately leads or sales.

At the same time as adding keywords or phrases for which you do want your ads to show, also add negative keywords, to block irrelevant searches, and those searching with the wrong intention. For example, if you are a car insurance provider excluding 'travel', 'home', 'life', 'claim' and 'job' type keywords will better ensure that your ad does not appear in searches that include those terms. Create a list in Excel so it can be easily imported into Google or Microsoft Ads accounts.

Create cut-through creative ideas

The difficulty with PPC advertising is that communication is dumbed down to a limited number of characters, the same text font, and colours. This limits a brand's ability to gain competitive advantage through creativity. There are however some marketing solutions to this paradox.

 Best Practice

Price comparison insurance website https://www.comparethemarket.com/ launched in 2009 featuring fictional Russian meerkat, Aleksandr Orlov. The ad campaign featured on British commercial TV. It centres on the character's frustration that people keep coming to his website https://www.comparethemeerkat.com/ looking for car insurance, not meerkats, as 'Market' sounds similar to 'Meerkat' when spoken in a Russian accent.

As the cost of establishing a branded URL is negligible, the campaign generates clicks to its site for a fraction of the cost of a click for 'car insurance'.

Building on the campaign's distinctive visual style and tone of voice, it has extended to selling soft toy meerkats as well as giving them away as a sales promotion incentive. Also, to promote/sponsor musical events (Meerkat Music), cinema nights out (Meerkat Movies), and discounted eating out (Meerkat Meals). All helps to maintain awareness of the insurance site.

By creating better branded communications and demand for your own searched for phrases it is therefore possible to limit reliance on mass and competitive search terms and establish your own route to market.

The digital world offers a growing range of multi-media opportunities. The social media platforms allow rich images to accompany text, and more nuanced targeting based on interests and media consumption, as well as behaviour and geography.

Further, while video sharing sites also allow video advertising, there is growing evidence that intrusive ads spoil what many see as leisure activity. Thus, viewers tend to just watch the first few seconds. YouTube now has a dual strategy to this conundrum. While it increasingly interrupts videos with ads, it also offers consumers advertising-free viewing at a price. Net, if you wish to advertise, you need to get your message across in a very short space of time. Nevertheless, for those with a viral seeking mindset, and who recognise, the ability to embed 'interesting' videos in other social media, free video hosting alone remains a benefit.

Understand where your advertising shows

Most recently there has been a furore about ads showing alongside 'politically incorrect' content. Thus, a number of prominent advertisers withdrew their advertising from some platforms. The lessons are clear; 'buyer beware' and 'look before you leap'. Despite Internet advertising accounting for a sizeable percentage of advertising spend, similarities with the 'wild west' remain with limited quality standards, proof of media substance, and little law enforcement.

At the time of writing the search engine advertising platforms such as Google Ads and Microsoft Advertising allow you choose whether your ad shows on their search platforms or via their extended content networks. They also enable 'remarketing' to those who have previously engaged with your advertising. Our experience suggests that advertising via the search engine platforms delivers higher click-through rates. However, functionality within the systems may also allow the 'ad savvy' to identify some websites that perform well for your brand.

Further, be aware that the default for Google, is that the content network is turned 'on'. You should turn it 'off' until you know what you are doing. It is better to run separate search and content network campaigns. The people your ads find through search are *seekers*. The people who find your ads on the content network are *readers!* And less likely to be buyers.

There are also several advertising software tools and networks such as Admixer, and PopAds, which assist with the planning and evaluation of campaigns. Thus, giving you extra control over where your ads show, and at what price per impression.

Measure comparative and absolute media effectiveness

The ultimate aim of marketing communication is to maximise consumer impressions or opportunities to see (cf. television ratings (TVRs) or gross rating points (GRPs)), maximise reach, at minimum cost per impression and sale. So do all you can to measure effectiveness, as well as relative performance across different media. The more you understand the better you'll be able to forward plan and deploy your budget.

Of course, the value of digital impressions varies considerably, and they lack the impact, and reach, of traditional media such as television. Though this has always been, and will always be, a key marketing variable. So when planning media campaigns, understand relative reach, and impact as well as impressions,.

Google is also aware of the limitations in online measurement and now operates 'Active View' on YouTube and some Display Network sites. Also 'Active GRP'. An 'Active View' occurs when a display ad 'is at least 50% viewable on the screen for at least 1 second' and when a video ad 'is at least 50% viewable on the screen for at least 2 seconds'. Active View, of course, cannot tell you whether the viewer is looking at the screen.

Active GRP, meanwhile, is the online equivalent of a standard GRP. It is the product of Active OTS (Opportunities to See) multiplied by percentage of the target demographic. Thus an Active GRP is a digital version of campaign reach and frequency, but unlike TV GRPs – lets advertisers react in real-time. On the plus side, the 'active' element provides added value versus a conventional TV GRP, whereas on the minus side, a one second view, is just one thirtieth of a typical TV GRP. Nielsen provides these data as a paid for service, though only in eight countries at the time of writing. (7)

So when measuring online advertising campaigns, don't just measure impressions, click-through-rates and cost. Also try and measure unique reach. Further, while reach may be difficult to establish, and is often relatively 'low', share of impressions provides a guide. If share approaches 100%, this suggests you are missing few click opportunities within the 'norms' for the medium as a whole.

The bottom line, is of course, to understand the effect on sales. But to measure this clearly, establish 'control' areas, for example, areas free of other media activity, to better establish the effect of investing in a specific medium.

Prominent digital and social media services

Beyond the textual limitations of Google there are a number of other digital media, in particular social media, that are more suited to leverage creativity and build brands. These include:

- online retailers, of which the most prominent are Amazon, and Ebay
- local business add-ons such as Google Business and Microsoft Business. The latter allows the import of data from the former, and both are important to boost local search prominence on maps, and work for searches such as 'hairdressers near me'.
- blogging platforms, where Wordpress is the most prominent
- messaging services, such as Whats App (owned by Facebook), Facebook Messenger, and iMessage (Apple)
- social media networking and content sharing platforms, of which Facebook is the largest.

For an up-to-date summary and indication of the reach of the expanding range of digital media, Alexa.com (8) and Wikipedia (9) and are good places to start.

Google and Facebook owned sites far surpass others in terms of online use accounting for 22% and 16% time respectively (10). They also command a combined 78% of online advertising spend. The next nearest in usage is music streaming site Spotify which accounts for 3% time. Some of the most prominent or interesting media are also summarised in Figure 31.6.

Some technologies worth highlighting include:

- location-based service provider Foursquare. This has spawned a range of business and consumer services that are useful to 'mortar' based businesses
- image sharing and sourcing platform, Flickr. Their 'commons catalogue' offers images with 'no known copyright' 'free of charge'. Though always check the small print!

Most digital services are US owned. Thus, unsurprisingly, they first built their user bases in the USA, before extending, initially to English speaking, and then other language speaking countries. Through commercialising their offers, they have enjoyed explosive stock market growth. As a result, the tech majors; Google, Amazon, Facebook, Apple and Microsoft (the so-called 'GAFAM'), are among the world's largest companies by market capitalisation. Understanding their acquisition behaviour provides insights on how they are commercialising their offers, to benefit brands and advertisers.

For example, having acquired Instagram, Facebook now allows Facebook only and combined Facebook and Instagram multi-media campaigns. Specifically, it allows businesses to set up business pages and boost posts or create and run ad campaigns (though presently from a personal account). It also allows highly nuanced targeting using multiple variables including gender, age, location, education level, relationship status, interests, behaviour and media consumption. You are also able to choose whether to buy impressions or clicks. While often 'good' value, if directing visitors to your website, do monitor the source, depth and outcome of visits independently too. Looking to the future, it would be unsurprising for some form of advertising to appear on their messaging system.

Other US owned media include Quora and Taboola. There are also many focused on the Chinese market including QQ and QZone.

Figure 31.6 *Applications, benefits and limitations of prominent digital and social media*

Digital Media	Application	Pros	Cons
Google Ads (USA)	Search engine advertising	Largest global search engine Increasing range of advertising options	Mainly text only ad medium
Microsoft Advertising (USA)	Search engine advertising	Default on Kindle Lower cost per click than Google	Lower reach than Google Text only ad medium
Amazon (USA)	Online retailer and advertising medium	World's largest online retailer Reach buyers not viewers Website users have higher purchase intent than Facebook or Google users Enables direct product sale, and also via your own shop Reaches a dozen or so major countries, though accounts operate independently	Complex fees system; charges for sales, services as a percentage of the selling price Separate fees for advertising Promotion sensitive
Ebay (USA)	Auction and shopping site	Enables auction and 'fixed price' selling via listings and advertising Able to create 'outlet' stores Integrates Paypal payment system	Complex fees system; charges for listings plus a percentage of the selling price Paypal charges fee for payment processing

Google Business (USA)	Local business add on	Boosts business profile Provides website option Helps you feature on local map searches Allows reviews and posts (helps boost rankings)	Partly a replacement for Google+ Posts disappear from the Google search page after c. 2 weeks
Wordpress (Automattic, USA)	Blogging and content management tool	One of the most popular and free online content i.e. website management tools Hosts over 1 in 3 websites Offers variety of design themes and templates Recently launched advertising service	Fees charged for advanced features Supports range of plugs with advanced features e.g. e-commerce
Tumblr (Automattic, USA)	Microblogging and social networking website	Hosts 475m blogs Many changes of ownership since launch in 2006, acquired by Automattic in 2019	Blog traffic waning at time of writing
Twitter (USA)	Social net-working and micro-blogging ser-vice	390m users SMS and short Internet video, allows embedded links Integrates with other websites e.g. blogs, LinkedIn, Features trending topics Supports multi-media ads	More adult user base Messages ('tweets') limited to 280 characters Response rates have fallen since their early days
Whats App (Facebook, USA)	Messaging	>2bn users Enables encrypted individual and group messaging and video sharing Enterprise version allows conversational customer service and e-commerce	Users require a smart phone, windows phones not supported Advertising not presently allowed, though ads from other media, can click to Whats App chats
Facebook (USA)	Personal social network	World's fourth highest traffic website/largest social networking site (2.2bn users) High daily usage Environment more suited to consumer brands Enables multi-media advertising and targeting by interests and behaviour Can buy impressions or clicks; cheaper than Google	Socially motivated rather than actively searching audience More female bias Less suited to b2b brands

YouTube (Google, USA)	Video sharing	World's second highest traffic website (>2bn users) Easy to embed video into other websites Video and on-screen text advertising medium	Risks of competitive advertising intrusion Only the first few seconds of an ad are viewed on average
Instagram (Facebook, USA)	Mobile image and video sharing app	>1bn users Allows photo and video sharing, storytelling via multiple social media platforms Also advertising, or influencer paid posts Creative and high quality image environment; thus suits aspirational and lifestyle brands	High young female, lower male following Users require a smart-phone
Tik Tok (China)	Video sharing networking app	800m users Allows video creation to 15 seconds, has spawned new viral trends Added new 'social gifting' feature in 2020; has prompted many beauty companies and brands to sign-up to use this feature Uses artificial intelligence to decide what to show viewers	Younger bias (40% are aged 16-24), slight male bias Subject to privacy, propaganda, addiction and bullying concerns President Trump has banned it in the USA unless it is US owned; Oracle and Walmart seem frontrunners to buy the US business.
Reddit (USA)	Social news aggregation, rating and discussion website	430m users Q&A forum, highly moderated, topics voted up and down High incidence of campaigning content Supports advertising	Over half users are US based, UK (7-8%), mainly male, tend to be more privacy concerned, and 'anti-establishment'
Snapchat (USA)	Camera and messaging app	400m users Provides tools and lens to customise and share videos/stories Allows advertising and targeting based on interests, behaviour and location Suits immediate messaging	Youth appeal, particularly under 16s Increasing incidence of porn activity

Pinterest (USA)	Pin board style social photo sharing	370m users Integrates/links to Twitter and Facebook Like a search engine for images/virtual shop front; consumers in planning mode Pictures better build brands & convey emotional benefits Supports buyable pins and catalogues	More female user base (60%) Some repetition in photo sharing Pinterest says *'anything you 'pin' to their site belongs to them. Completely. Wholly. Forever and for always'*
LinkedIn (USA)	Business-related social network	World's largest business networking site, 310m users Allows posts to business or interest groups, also ability to send personalised messages to individuals Multi-media advertising medium; ability to target by sector, country	Interest group content spam like, though you can now block messages coming into your inbox Fees charged for advanced features
Foursquare City Guide and Swarm (USA)	Location-based mobile apps	City Guide is a local search and discovery app; allows brands to create pages of 'tips', encourage followers, recommendations, and offer promoted updates Swarm is the original social networking and discovery app, allows users to check-in and find friends Provide 2 business promotion products; Places (database of 105m places) and Pinpoint (mobile user base of 150m) Allows user targeting by visit history, taste preferences and demographics	Mainly US based Users require a smart-phone Only superusers can edit venue information
Flickr (SmugMug, USA)	Image hosting and sharing	87m users Rich resource of creative commons i.e. free as well as purchasable images	Popularity waning Need to click on specific images to verify their rights status Image search functionality is more limited than some commercial providers

A key issue to national Governments with the rise of the tech majors is that vast sums of economic output are sent offshore, thus reducing domestic productivity, and local tax takes. Several countries therefore, most notably the UK, plan to levy extra tax on income earned as well as profits. At the time of writing, two of the tech majors, say these taxes, will be passed on to their customers. In other words, the business seller or advertiser will ultimately pay. The USA is also considering anti-trust legislation.

Success factors for social media marketing

Understand social media specifics

Social media counters the textual and colour limitations of search and PPC. Yet each individual platform has its own audience, and sub-message. They are far from the same. From the consumers' point of view, the role of social media is to socialise, yet also entertain, share information, build relationships, show-off and more. Thus, brands must understand the media, the behavioural and cultural norms, and select those that meet their marketing aims, and brand strategy. So, at the outset, understand the audiences, and the sub-messages. Cross platform usage can be better controlled by creating and defining your own customer targets which can then be applied to each platform. Also check out where your competitors are and learn from what they are doing.

Re-assert and re-work the brand

To cut-through, without the benefit of an expensive TV commercial on which to anchor your brand, your campaign must suit the medium and be implemented consistently. Not simply in name and logo terms but in a rounded, fully functional way that reflects the media channel, meets consumer needs, and enhances the brand values and consumers' own experiences.

Remember too, that the strongest brands deliver emotional benefits and build strong relationships with customers. Consequently aim to provide more convenient services, and content to add-value. You will not have missed that the digital marketing world is awash with *10 ways to... the 6 most compelling reasons to* ... and so on. Also consider providing entertainment, education, inspiration, and social interaction. All build bonds and encourage consumer usage, loyalty, and ultimately endorsement and advocacy.

Listen and respond quickly

Social media is fast-paced, ever-changing, and highly interactive. At any given moment someone could be saying something about your product and brand. This presents both opportunities and threats. It also means that brands have to listen to communications and have policies to respond in an agile and meaningful manner. Sometimes, in minutes. See *Chapter 28 Crisis Planning and Management* for insights on how to anticipate and manage risks.

28▶

Think logically and laterally to create winning communications ideas

The trouble with many products and services is that they do not provide the sexiest communication material. However quality content is more important than posting regularly. So do create and post distinctive material but don't set quantity targets. Start by planning a promotional programme, for example, based on 'new news', product launches, events and the seasons.

While everyone wants every campaign to go 'viral' this is not something that is easily planned for and designed. There are, however, lessons to learn from successful campaigns. Customers tend to share content that resonates with them, such as stories and jokes. Thus, successful campaigns often tend to be the least branded, topical and humourous. Check out what's worked previously, what's on-trend, and try to lead the pack. Ideas will follow from insights that others do not have; through listening, observing, and of course, research. This is at the heart of being a Marketing Director.

Maximise endorsements

Customers are swayed by recommendations and reviews particularly from experts and trusted sources. Indeed, 'likes' and 'ratings' are an integral part of the digital ecosystem. They are also valued by search engines. So work proactively and transparently to encourage endorsements.

Endorsements are so important in the digital ecosystem such that they have also spawned a new type of marketing - influencer marketing. Influencers abound across the web, and those with the greatest followings, are deemed most influential. Many have quickly become rich on the back of paid for endorsements. Some have even been hired by television companies to boost the credibility and reach of their programmes.

Today, influencer activities therefore span 'unpaid' and 'paid' recommendations and thus regulations now require influencers to make clear what is paid for (and thus considered advertising).

It also means that public relations has a powerful role to play in the marketing mix. However, make sure that it is measureable, within budget, and matches your brand strategy.

In context, influencer endorsements are really a form of traditional 'word of mouth' marketing. So when engaging in this kind of activity remember that there are many other forms including personal display, sampling, and sales. 'Word of mouth' also extends to local community, charity and sports promotion including gifting and sponsorship.

 Best Practice

Blendtec is a US brand of food blender. In 2007 it created an Internet sensation with a YouTube video featuring its Chief Executive, Tom Dickson, dropping an iPhone into a blender, pushing the smoothie button, and grinding the product to dust. This video has been viewed over 12m times and some even more times (11). The 'Will it Blend?' series now runs to over 180 episodes and involves the destruction of diverse objects including Justin Bieber CDs, credit cards and golf balls. Watch them all at https://www.willitblend.com.

Measure and manage

In *Chapter 5 Setting Objectives and Measuring Marketing* we discussed 'what gets measured gets managed'. There are many online articles on what to measure and the most used social media metrics are visitors and sources of traffic, network size, quantity and quality of product commentary, search engine ranking, leads generated, and influence. Reach, impressions, sales conversion and ROI should be top of your list.

B2C vs. B2B Marketing

Marketing a product to an individual consumer rather than to a business is often a very different proposition. Or is it? The growth of digital media means that there are an increasing number of channels and methods from which to choose. So how should marketers approach the task of engaging and winning customers? It's a bit like learning a dance.

Figure 31.7 *The differences between b2b and b2c marketing*

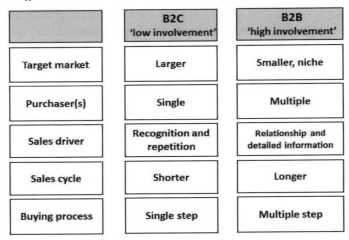

	B2C 'low involvement'	B2B 'high involvement'
Target market	Larger	Smaller, niche
Purchaser(s)	Single	Multiple
Sales driver	Recognition and repetition	Relationship and detailed information
Sales cycle	Shorter	Longer
Buying process	Single step	Multiple step

Businesses that sell to consumers

The challenge of B2C marketing is to build product awareness and convert browsers into buyers. As it's usually a 'low involvement' purchase, say to buy a confectionery bar, marketing campaigns must capture the consumer's interest immediately. Typically, mass promotion activities like TV and press advertising are employed. In addition, special offers such as discounts or vouchers help 'activate' the purchase. The challenge is thus to establish an effective one-step routine.

In the online world, multiple factors influence consumers to click and buy, and Google's own research suggests that consumers continuously research and evaluate options. In effect, this means they are also continuously short-listing and deselecting options before deciding to buy. Influencing factors include the category and competitive context, thus the strength of benefits, recommendations, immediacy of delivery, as well as incentives (6). The purchasing process must also minimise barriers to sales. In particular, be simple and easy, for example, by integrating the shopping basket and checkout page. Any more than a couple of clicks and the customer will go to another shop.

Businesses that sell to businesses

The goal of B2B marketing is also to convert prospects into customers but the purchase is usually more considered. More decision makers are usually involved, and the challenge is to engage and educate the target audience and build relationships. To succeed a B2B company must generate and nurture leads over a longer time period. A careless or quick step could mean a lost partner (or customer). Your challenge is therefore to establish an effective multi-step relationship building routine.

In the online world, an email campaign or online advertising campaign can drive prospects to a website but is less likely to achieve an immediate sale. The eventual goal should be to secure a meeting with a sales representative in order to discuss the customer's businesses requirements in more detail and guide him, her or them to completion of the sale. By providing information about the products and services, benefits, features, possibly pricing, and contact information the customer can be reassured and his or her trust won. Conceiving marketing activity as one of several steps in a longer, integrated, multi-step campaign that includes awareness and relationship building via direct mail, newsletters, video promotion, webinars, virtual exhibitions, conferences or live events and social media such as Twitter or LinkedIn will be more likely to persuade. Today many use Customer Relationship Management programs. There are many to choose from, including the mighty Salesforce and Marketo, to more lowly and less costly offerings. There are also software providers that provide contact details on visitors to websites such as Visitor Queue and Kissmetrics.

Email marketing

Digital communication and cloud computing capabilities provide many extra marketing benefits over and above direct mail. This often starts with customer relationship management (CRM) *(which we examine in detail in Chapter 18)*. Which basically combines existing marketing and sales data with context on individual customers.

18

The ability to email many people at relatively low cost means that contact has been transformed with better targeting and use of digital media. Coupled with more efficient firewalls, spam has been reduced dramatically, and the opt-in nature of online practice has enabled a more powerful promotion and relationship building channel. In both the B2C and B2B worlds this also gives *sales* extra impetus.

There are many proprietary email platforms which allow both creation of customised content and database management. Examples include Mail Chimp, Constant Contact and Email Octopus. Most providers offer a free service layer to allow you to run tests before scaling up activity. The beauty of these services is that they also provide metrics on email arrivals, bounces (incorrect email addresses), email opens, and click-through-rates. They also offer website plug-ins to allow website visitors to sign-up to your mailing list when visiting your website, and while complying with data protection regulations.

Where to start

Buying or building a sales database from prospect to customer has led to a new process that sits between marketing and sales. The process is called 'nurturing'. The idea is to identify who you want to do business with, then through the database, build a regular useful relationship so sales can intervene when an opportunity arises.

'Nurturing' (Figure 31.8) recognizes that the sales triggers are often beyond the influence of *sales*. This therefore demands a programme of activity with customised collateral. Understanding how search works in conjunction with new software applications enables leads from web sites being better identified both from source and the way the website is constructed.

Figure 31.8 *Nurturing - a graphical explanation*

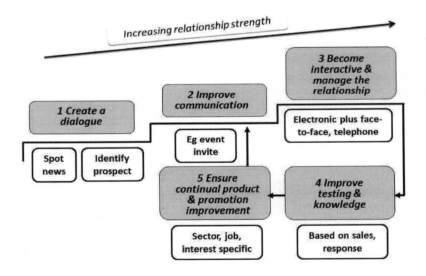

For this to be effective the system has to be maintained with accurate promotion activity and timely response information and feedback to and from the sales force.

Marketing collateral should be geared to specific communication objectives at all stages in the relationship building process, for example, online information enquiry, telephone call, to first purchase, service request and complaint. By combining low weight contact and active database management, the effectiveness of the face-to-face sales activity improves, and costs reduce.

When a prospect becomes a customer, purchases inform the subsequent messages and offers promoted, to help 'nurture' the relationship and drive loyalty.

Automating the process helps your sales colleagues be more proactive too. Ensuring comprehensive and mutual understanding will also enhance the preparation of collateral material, inspire more relevant and timely communications to sustain interest, build trust to generate inbound enquiries and close sales.

In B2C, packs and promotions are digitally purchased, sold and managed by retailers. This means a content management system should also become part of your plan. Work closely with internal company functions, including IT, HR as well as sales to capture and make the most of these opportunities.

Information management is usually the province of IT. Many Chief Information Officers (CIOs) have historically been protective, often understandably so, as the robustness and usability of data is vital to the whole of the organisation. Yet marketing's role is to translate the data into information on which customer and investment decisions can be made.

Mobile applications

A mobile application or app is software or a computer programme designed to run on a mobile phone, tablet or watch.

While many are installed as standard, they are also downloadable from distributors most notably Google (Play Store), Apple (App Store) and Microsoft (Microsoft Store). Many are free of charge and others are paid for, with the proceeds split between the app creator and the distributor.

The range and functionality of apps now means that apps work as a promotion tool and/or a service and thus source of income. The massive growth in mobile penetration and number of apps is such that the global market is worth nearly $600bn (12). Some apps originated as a short-cut to browsing the Internet, thus ease of use is generally a key benefit.

Types of app

There are three main types of app:

- Native app; these are specific to, and tend to perform better on a particular platform such as Apple, Android (Google) or Windows (Microsoft)

- Web-based app; these are coded using common web code such as HTML, CSS or Javascript. Personal databases are stored on servers and thus Internet access is needed for a smooth user experience, and

- Hybrid app; these are coded using a single code which works on multiple mobile platforms.

The open-source nature of (some of) the digital world means that lots of tools and code are available to develop apps. This has therefore spawned an industry of tools and app developers.

App development

For the marketer considering developing an app you should view this as an innovation challenge that relies on IT expertise. Thus at the outset create a clear specification of your needs, and desired functions. Then bear in mind, and mitigate the pitfalls inherent in most IT system development.

 ## Pitfalls to Avoid

Failing to meet customer needs

As discussed in *Chapter 23, New Product and Service Development*, the number one reason why new products and services fail is because they fail to meet customer needs. This is particularly the case with new technology which is often simply a collection of features seeking a need. So don't fall into the trap of supply-push app development; involve customers throughout the process. Understand their needs, attitudes, product selection criteria and alternatives. Also use stimuli to provoke new insights on your ideas, what's important and not. All increases the chance of finding an unmet or new need, and thus boosting your venture.

Trying to do too much

One clear lesson from the Coronovirus pandemic is the early and failed promises of track and tracing apps. This is also a common challenge in any hefty and expensive IT development. It is difficult for anyone to see yet alone understand the big picture, and thus manage effectively.

Thus the agile marketing director should aim low not high. So first design and deliver an app with basic functionality, and prove that this resonates with customers and users. In so doing you should also prove your basic business case.

Then second, evolve the functionality in small steps, and prove that this also resonates with customers and users. And above all, don't just rely on customer click behaviour, get out there and talk to them.

Throughout view development as a series of steps, all with the customer front and centre, and matched to a clear and specific business case. This in itself will help de-risk your development project.

(Lack of) money, money, money

Further, if you are creating an app, or business from scratch, finance will be a very big issue. A good place to start in this respect is to read George Berkowski's *How to Build a Billion Dollar App*.

Integrated marketing

Integrated marketing is where all activity is brought together under a single creative banner or campaign in order to convey a consistent message and ensure a clear customer take-out. Integration requires recognition of the actual role of each medium, and coordination of messages across all parts of the marketing mix.

TV advertising is often the most impactful and effective medium to convey the core brand message, and emotional benefits, while other media are better at explaining specific products, product features, customer service benefits, and supporting more targeted local activity and promotions.

 Best Practice

Honda is a company built on dreams in the belief that this will lead to new insights, revolutionary new technologies in automobiles, motorcycles, power products, parts and other fields of mobility. They aim to be a company that society wants to exist by creating new value, exceeding expectations and solving global environmental challenges.

Honda's 'World of Dreams' advertising echoes these beliefs and communicates the benefits to customers (13). TV conveys over-arching brand benefits, while local dealer promotion activity focuses on specific models and customer groups.

Success factors for integrated (digital) marketing

By way of a summary here is a list of key factors to integrate your digital and broader marketing activities successfully:

Embrace digital for itself

Digital marketing can change the role of each element in the marketing mix. It can enhance your product or service as well as inspire a very wide range of promotion opportunities. Start by considering the additional benefits that digital can add to your product or brand proposition. Potential benefits include, paper-free delivery, paper-free billing, savings on storage and cost, better control or personal management, education, entertainment and social benefits.

Change your view of individual media to see their role in the whole

The fundamental questions are... *what channel is the most effective for what message?* And *what combination will best reach my audience and generate sales at the lowest cost?*

It's a mistake to think of digital as a series of techniques and media platforms. Consider everything as digital and make your web site *'Marketing Central'*. Every day new technological advances inspire new product/service delivery and promotion opportunities. For example, mobile phones and tablets have changed the nature of email communication, reading and staying in touch. Cloud computing will reduce the cost of storing information remotely, and inspire a further drift to a paper-free, multi-media rich world. Changes in consumer behaviour such as simultaneous watching TV and online surfing are prompting big TV advertisers to coordinate TV advertising and online activity.

Consider ways to combine media to increase message impact and activate extra sales. Easy ways to do this are to promote your website url via all forms of advertising. It is also relatively easy to integrate social media sites, so for example, a blog post or tweet is then automatically re-promoted via other social media.

Re-define your brand in terms of its digital presence in graphics and copy

Communication activity will be better integrated if it all follows from an overarching creative idea born of the brand and its emotional values. In other words, a creative 'campaign' theme and style.

Plan and deliver consistent communications over a long time period

Ensure consistent implementation through all media and over time via a series of campaigns, each with a finite start and stop. Avoid the temptation to change the creative lead too frequently as it risks customer confusion. Many elements of digital marketing also require strong creative controls and monitoring to ensure consistent communications.

Build strategies and plans based on superior consumer understanding

Successful marketing implementation stems from competitive marketing strategies covering the entire marketing mix. Robust consumer insights provide a foundation to get the basics right and also give you an edge. OFCOM is a good source of general UK data, though commission research to understand issues and opportunities specific to your brand.

 ## Where to start

Once you've developed your creative materials, work backwards from your desired financial outcomes, to determine the required customer outcomes. To do this, you'll need to understand the metrics behind customer journey. In the simplest of terms, to determine;

- how many customers must see an advertisement for your product in order to try it? Then,
- how many must try it before someone buys it.

The answers to these questions allow you to derive audience awareness, conversion from awareness to click-through, trial or enquiry, and also conversion from click-through, trial or enquiry to purchase ratios. Or alternatively from plain awareness to purchase. This is the so-called 'objective and task method'.

The second step in the process is to short-list potential media, both digital and otherwise, in terms of their ability to reach your target market. Then do the maths on which media give the most cost effective combination of impressions, to achieve your desired customer outcomes. Throughout, you may have to make some initial judgement calls on the relative performance of each medium (or at least until you have some test results to go on).

Finally, test your way from low investment to higher investment levels. By testing and learning as you go, you'll not only optimise the performance of your campaign, but potentially save or help make millions of pounds. This is the essence of professional marketing and the stuff careers are made of.

Marketing automation

One of the major drawbacks of digital marketing and in particular social media marketing is that it is *highly* time intensive; communication is much more individual and personal rather than mass targeted. Like website development and management it requires manpower to create, upload, distribute and manage content, monitor communications and specifically engage in direct individual communication.

The devil is in the detail. We know of some savvy 'twenty somethings' that always research insightful or humourous content. So search the web for inspiration. And then hone your words, and check with others that your ideas resonate. Allow at least half an hour per post per medium.

In some businesses, such as Dell, social interaction is the responsibility of many individuals. In other organisations it is the preserve of few.

Fortunately, there are an increasing number of tools, and many free tools to help manage and automate social media marketing (14). Among the tools available, Hootsuite, Socialoomph and Tweetdeck, allow you to schedule updates to other platforms such as Facebook, LinkedIn, Google Business and Twitter. They also allow you to schedule activity and manage followers. These tools, and others such as Klout (now part of Brandwatch), also enable social media monitoring.

Marketing and sales integration

An additional challenge, for those businesses, that generate leads, and sell products and services, is how to manage the handover from marketing to sales. Also how to track and nurture leads. At the most basic level, Microsoft tools, such as Outlook, Excel, Word, and Access provide useful functionality. These also work together to help send emails, track responses, and capture and store key information. These software can also be stored in the cloud, for example, via OneNote, so several people can access, maintain and use the same data. These tools are most suited to smaller businesses with small numbers of customers, and smaller numbers of team members needing to access and manage these data.

Larger businesses with higher volumes of marketing activity, leads, and customers require more powerful functionality. There is a growing industry of software providers and consulting firms available to help. Salesforce offers off-the-shelf enterprise software; this can also be customised to needs, though is at the expensive end of the price spectrum. At the other end of the price spectrum, there are some providers, such as Bitrix; they provide a free and basic single user offer.

Project management

There are also a growing number of tools to help manage tasks or projects and automate processes. Asana, Trello, Slack and Basecamp are options to manage tasks. Process Bliss is an example of software that you can use to automate pretty much any process. All offer either free trial or free entry level solutions.

Organising the marketing function

The world of digital means there are more elements to manage both strategically and operationally. Also more media to juggle to establish the most cost-effective or profitable combination. However, digital has also relegated the ability of the Marketing Director to see the big picture, and invest for best returns. So do not be seduced by simply structuring your marketing department to support digital marketing.

Moreover, structure your marketing department to meet the aims of the business, and leverage key business drivers. How you do this should follow from the business strategy, and your CEO's and Board's priorities. Whether to save costs, retain the status-quo, drive customer growth or business and brand value. Through a process of change, or as a new hire, present options together with their pros and cons, as well as champion, what you could do to best serve the business.

In the event of moral dilemmas, remain calm, and practical.

There are main three ways to organise your in-house team to maximise benefits, though a hybrid of more than one may be most opportune:

I. By customer group, category, product or brand

Businesses competing in the most competitive markets tend to structure by customer group, category, or brand. This is because customer understanding and brands are key businesses drivers. This type of structure is particularly useful to accumulate customer segment and market understanding and also build brands. It works when you have more than one sizeable brand in a category, with each occupying different positioning spaces.

2. By marketing activity or customer outcomes

Businesses with high volumes of complex or specialist marketing work may structure by the type of work undertaken. Examples, include pricing and merchandising in retail, research or data analysis, in companies collecting or dealing with large amounts of data.

At the outset gain a comprehensive understanding of your customer's journey and triggers, drivers and barriers to discovering your brand, purchasing, using and repeat purchasing your brand. This will provide insights on what are the most important activities to undertake.

Some organisations organise teams to focus on customer acquisition and retention, though if you do this, you should also make sure someone retains the overview on return on investment over the customer lifecycle.

3. By type of digital media activity, channel, or medium

We estimate that there are over two dozen different digital disciplines, from website development, to search engine optimisation (SEO), search engine marketing (SEM) or pay-per-click advertising, to social media planning and optimisation, community management, video production and so on. Some require particular design or technical skills such as HTML, CSS or JavaScript coding.

In the early days of the Internet, IT departments set-up, and many still do manage websites. Though successful marketing today requires a blend of IT technical skills and customer know-how. IT departments often provide the former and marketing or research departments the latter.

Today you also have a choice to hire on an 'ad hoc' basis or hire in. What's best depends on the scale of challenge, and whether you have a start-up or maintenance need. If hiring on an 'ad hoc' basis, there are many IT specialists for hire in the management consulting and agency sector.

In the long term though, there are benefits in building in-house capabilities in order to boost measurement and management agility, and value for money. As we enter the fourth decade of the Internet, there are more specialist and educated technical skills available. Though for the most part there remains a clear divide in skills between the technical and marketing, and few experts in both. However, small businesses can take solace in website development and maintenance being easier with the likes of Wordpress which is both intuitive and offers a range of plug-ins.

Influencer marketing is a growing specialism though best 'focused' by brand. So choose influencers that match your niche. Buzz Sumo is a good place to start. Then when approaching them, remember that influencing is their profession. So be personal, and ask about and agree rates first.

The frequency of outpourings from Google, other media and commentators also takes some keeping up with. So if your department is large enough, consider a *technical marketing executive* to act as a 'watch person' and liaison between the technical and marketing.

Though whatever you do, it also helps to maintain agency relationships for specialist know-how.

Managing digital marketing

Management is best facilitated through accurate customer understanding, setting clear objectives, and measurement. By establishing clear customer and financial outcomes then allows marketing planning and investment by platform or medium to deliver the desired outcomes.

While each medium provides performance data in and of itself, throughout, aim for a common set of metrics, across the organisation, and agencies, in order to compare relative marketing investment returns.

Your aim throughout is to be platform neutral, manage the budget, and remain vigilant to issues and opportunities in order to invest ever more wisely. Thus shift investment to the best performing media. Of course, this is not easy.

Digital means data and data is the province of your Information Technology (IT) department. So work with your IT director to establish what data is held, and how to best collate and use it to make the best marketing decisions.

Compiling accurate and up-to-date information allows the establishment of a 'marketing dashboard' – a snapshot of current response information compared to activity and costs, all mapped to budgets. Information reported should mirror the metrics established to manage your business. For a brief reminder on how to do this, take another look at *Chapter 5 - Setting Objectives and Measuring Marketing Performance*. Combining external information, such as simple Google or Twitter keyword alerts can provide additional insights, sources of competitive advantage or 'early warning radar'.

Regular formal reporting and meetings will also uncover and cross-pollinate learning, forge accountability, maintain standards and reduce duplication.

 ## Pitfalls to Avoid

The digital world is awash with pitfalls, from data short-comings, to security breaches and losses. All present reputation threats in varying degrees.

Disaster recovery

Thus it is incumbent to have recovery plans in place for all eventualities. And in particular, to ensure a very rapid response given the pace at which information travels in the digital world.

Though prevention is better than a cure. So again work with your IT director to maintain a secure data environment, and comply with data protection regulations. All organisations controlling and processing information must comply with data processing regulations. In the UK, the Information Commissioner's Office (ICO) is responsible for upholding information rights in the public interest. They have a number of guides, services and tools to help organisations comply with data protection regulations. Data controllers should also register with the ICO.

For a refresher on managing and mitigating risks work through *Chapter 28 on Crisis Planning and Management.*

28▶

The future role of marketing

As we write the Coronavirus pandemic has engulfed us all. It's catastrophic events have challenged all organisations, and some will never be the same. However, challenges present opportunities, and this is where marketing should come to the fore. There are two key ways.

Firstly, by understanding customer behaviour, and thus the business implications and opportunities arising. Secondly, by presenting the business, and brand, in a positive light, and to capitalise on the identified opportunities.

While the future is unknown it is knowable. Marketing is the business function that understands customers and drives growth which means the future is yours.

In less than 6 months, it seems that the world has been catapulted further into a digital age. By understanding and extrapolating the forces at work helps envision the future. Do this to try and remain a step ahead. Take a look at *Chapter 21 - Creativity and Problem Solving* for more specific insights on how.

21▶

Key points to remember

1. Digital has changed the world forever; it gives provides more media channels to manage, and more opportunities for adding value to products. However the eternal challenge to boost brand performance, while managing the money remains. The role of the marketing director, therefore, is to remain media neutral and simply invest where you can to assuage customers most profitably.

2. Underlying this your role is also to hunt for new growth opportunities, lead innovation, embrace and drive change and build the culture. To do this you must be a 'business futurist', provide the strategic overview, and balance technology with better customer understanding, the many channels and overall needs of the brand.

3. This is all consistent with establishing 'early warning radar' on which the business can rely. There is potential competitive advantage in understanding, anticipating and planning for the future. So expect more mobility, more devices, more bandwidth and more inter-connected applications. Understand the constantly changing technology, watch and learn from competitors, plot the trends and forces, anticipate where changes and opportunities lie and keep experimenting.

4. Understand customers, their needs and digital behaviour. Generation Alpha (those born after around 2010) will be the most 'digitally savvy' yet. Customers also have an increasing interest and role in what we do. They combine into powerful groups affecting countries and companies alike. So put customers and their needs at the heart of what you do. This requires comprehensive research.

5. Appreciate the 'wisdom of crowds' and expect the 'flow of flocks'. Watch and plan to respond quickly as swarms swirl massively and suddenly, though momentarily, to injustices or simple human interest. This means understanding and preparing plans to mitigate risks, and grasp emerging opportunities quickly. Response time can be a bane or boon to your brand.

6. Develop more strategic and tailored customer relationships by focusing on the overall experience, embracing new distribution and promotion platforms and expanding revenue models.

7. Think like a media brand. Create content to complement and add value to your products and services. It will also be a magnet to attract customers.

8. Use the wealth of free analytical tools from Google, and others, to understand what works on your website, and where there is scope for improvement. Then make few and small changes, and monitor the effect. You won't go far wrong with a gradual process of continuous improvement.   But be afraid of large leaps; especially with new technology.

9. The apparent surfeit of data and seemingly accurate ROIs will often satisfy

the board's constant demand for empirical information, but this belies the actual costs of digital activity. The marketing director must remember the 'big' picture and collect and rely on robust data. So compare like with like data, understand media reach and impressions, and measure impact on the 'bottom line'.

10. Use your creativity and problem solving ability to stay focused on the customer, create cut-through solutions and build your brand. While the digital world may change, these skills remain as important as ever.

11. A mixture of internal departments and external agencies will help you stay ahead of the game. When searching for external agencies seek out those with technical *and* marketing skills.

12. Don't be afraid of experimenting, but test your way forward to better secure your fortune.

References and Further Reading

Introduction
References

1. https://www.themarketingdirectors.co.uk/role-of-marketing/

Chapter 31 Managing Digital Marketing
References

1. https://www.worldwidewebsize.com
2. https://netmarketshare.com Google has a 70% share for desktop/laptop searches and 94% share for mobile searches (year to August 2020)
3. Wiki is an online encyclopaedia, named after the Hawaiian word for fast. Wikis are powered by wiki software, created by Ward Cunningham called WikiWikiWeb, backacronymed to 'what I know is'
4. A squeeze page is a single website landing page designed for a specific promotion purpose and to capture customers' email contact details. Arnold, John; Lurie, Ian; Dickinson, Marty; Marsten, Elizabeth; Becker, Michael;*Web Marketing All-in-One Desk Reference For Dummies* (2012)
5. Google search engine optimisation starter guide: https://support.google.com/webmasters/answer/7451184?hl=en
6. Google Australia/New Zealand research, Decoding how consumers make purchase decisions, May 2020. https://www.thinkwithgoogle.com/intl/en-aunz/consumer-insights/consumer-journey/decoding-how-consumers-make-purchase-decisions
7. Nielsen Digital Ad Ratings reports https://support.google.com/campaignmanager/answer/6131068
8. https://www.alexa.com/topsites summarises the top 500 websites
9. https://en.wikipedia.org/wiki/Social_media provides a mini history and up-to-date summary of the reach of the major social media networks
10. OFCOM Online Nation 2020. Base all UK online adults 18+. https://www.ofcom.org.uk/__data/assets/pdf_file/0027/196407/online-nation-2020-report.pdf

11. https://www.youtube.com/watch?v=qg1ckCkm8YI
12. https://www.statista.com/statistics/269025/worldwide-mobile-app-revenue-forecast/
13. https://www.honda.co.uk/cars/world-of-honda/past/the-power-of-dreams.html
14. https://blog.hubspot.com/blog/tabid/6307/bid/29340/how-to-automate-your-social-media-marketing-like-the-pros.aspx

Recommended Reading

1. Arnold, John; Lurie, Ian; Dickinson, Marty; Marsten, Elizabeth; Becker, Michael;*Web Marketing All-in-One Desk Reference For Dummies*, 2012
2. Berkowski, George; *How to Build a Billion Dollar App*, 2014
3. Diamond, Stephanie; *Digital Marketing All in One for Dummies*, 2019
4. Miller, Dave; *Social Media Marketing*, 2020

Appendix 2

Acronyms

4G	fourth generation broadband cellular network technology
5G	fifth generation broadband cellular network technology
AMP	accelerated mobile pages
B2B	business to business
B2C	business to consumer
CEO	chief executive officer
CFO	chief financial officer
CIO	chief information officer
CRM	customer relationship management
CSS	cascading style sheets
CTR	click-through-rate
GAFAM	Google, Amazon, Facebook, Apple and Microsoft
GPS	global positioning satellite
GRPs	gross rating point
HD	high-definition
HTML	hypertext markup language
HTTPS	hypertext transfer protocol secure
ICO	Information Commissioner's Office
IT	Information Technology
OTS	opportunity-to-see
PPC	pay-per-click
ROI	return on investment
SEM	search engine marketing
SEO	search engine optimisation
SMS	short message service
SSL	secure sockets layer
TLS	transport layer security
TVRs	television rating
URL	uniform resource locator
WWW	worldwide web

Index

About The Marketing Director's Handbook

The Marketing Director's Handbook is the definitive practical guide for anyone managing a marketing function. It is truly unique:

- In a single reference source it contains practical advice, ideas, arguments and strategies to enhance the profitable growth and value of your organisation.
- Structured to help you lead a marketing department, undertake key marketing activities and solve marketing problems. All 30 chapters are usefully labelled by the type of job/activity that they'll help readers to undertake.
- Contains a comprehensive range of tools and models reflecting best market-place practices to help structure and enhance your thinking.
- Concise, jargon free and easy-to-read, use, digest, and refer to again after again.
- Jam-packed with best practice insights and ideas. Unconventionally, it focuses on practical learning points, all brought to life with anecdotes and visuals.

Our Offer to You

If you have purchased *The Marketing Director's Handbook Volume 2 - Managing digital marketing* via any channel, we offer you a hardback edition of the original The Marketing Director's Handbook, for just £36.99 (including free postage to UK addresses, though postage is extra to overseas addresses).

This offer is only available for direct orders from The Marketing Directors Ltd. To redeem this offer, just send your proof of purchase to handbook@themarketingdirectors.co.uk, and we'll then send you a link to buy the book.